I0476039

How To Get Ready To Give The Perfect Speech

What Tools To Use To Create Your Next Speech So That Your Message Will Be Remembered Forever!

"Practical, proven techniques that will help you to make your next speech a success"

Dr. Jim Anderson

Published by:
Blue Elephant Consulting
Tampa, Florida

Printed in the United States of America

Library of Congress Control Number: 2017902444

ISBN-13: 978-1543141146
ISBN-10: 1543141145

Warning – Disclaimer

The purpose of this book is to educate and entertain. This book does not promise or guarantee that anyone following the ideas, tips, suggestions, techniques or strategies will be hired. It is the discretion of employers if you will or will not be hired. The author, publisher and distributor(s) shall have neither liability nor responsibility to anyone with respect to any loss or damage caused, or alleged to be caused, directly or indirectly by the information contained in this book.

Recent Books By The Author

Product Management

- Manage Your Customers, Manage Your Product: Techniques For Product Managers To Better Understand What Their Customers Really Want

- Managing Your Product Manager Career: How Product Managers Can Find And Succeed In The Right Job

Public Speaking

- Creating Speeches That Work: How To Create A Speech That Will Make Your Message Be Remembered Forever!

- How To Organize A Speech In Order To Make Your Point: How to put together a speech that will capture and hold your audience's attention

CIO Skills

- How CIOs Can Bring Business And IT Together: How CIOs Can Use Their Technical Skills To Help Their Company Solve Real-World Business Problems

- New IT Technology Issues Facing CIOs: How CIOs Can Stay On Top Of The Changes In The Technology That

Powers The Company

IT Manager Skills

- How IT Managers Can Use New Technology To Meet Today's IT Challenges: Technologies That IT Managers Can Use In Order to Make Their Teams More Productive

- How To Build High Performance IT Teams: Tips And Techniques That IT Managers Can Use In Order To Develop Productive Teams

Negotiating

- The Art Of Packaging A Negotiation: How To Develop The Skill Of Assembling Potential Trades In Order To Get The Best Possible Outcome

- Getting What You Want In A Negotiation By Learning How To Signal: How To Develop The Skill Of Effective Signaling In A Negotiation In Order To Get The Best Possible Outcome

Miscellaneous

- How To Heal A Broken Leg – Fast!: Understanding how to deal with a broken leg in order to start walking again quickly

- How Software Defined Networking (SDN) Is Going To Change Your World Forever: The Revolution In Network Design And How It Affects

Note: See a complete list of books by Dr. Jim Anderson at the back of this book.

Acknowledgements

Any book like this one is the result of years of real-world work experience. In my over 25 years of working for 7 different firms, I have met countless fantastic people and I've been mentored by some truly exceptional ones. Although I've probably forgotten some of the people who made me the person that I am today, here is my attempt to finally give them the recognition that they so truly deserve:

- Thomas P. Anderson
- Art Puett
- Bobbi Marshall
- Bob Boggs

Dr. Jim Anderson

This book is dedicated to my wife Lori. None of this would have been possible without her love and support.

Thanks for the best years of my life (so far)...!

Speaking.   Negotiating.   Managing.   Marketing.

Table Of Contents

Getting Ready For A Speech Takes Time

Before we can give the perfect speech, we have to get ready to give the perfect speech. Just saying the words of our speech over and over again is a good first step, but it's not enough. We need to know what else we have to do prior to giving a speech in order to be ready when the big day comes.

We need to understand that how we feel during the delivery of our speech is going to play a big role in how our audience feels about our speech. The more enthusiasm that you can bring to your speech, then the more excited your audience is going to be to hear what you have to say. During your speech you'll need to be careful to pick your words carefully. The one thing that you don't want to do is to use any "filler words" that don't have to be there.

Every speech that we give is a performance. There are speakers out there that we recognize as being excellent speakers. We can model how they deliver their speeches in order to become more like them. At the same time, in order to make sure that our performance is top notch, we should consider taking some acting lessons so that our performance wows our audience.

Every speech that we give is different. Our speeches that have a question and answer section need to be very carefully created. We're going to have to be ready to give the answers that our audience will be looking for. Other types of speeches, such as debates, require us to prepare for them using completely different tactics.

The most powerful tool that any of us will have during a speech is time. We need to understand how to use this tool to allow us to fully communicate our message. If we don't use it well, then we won't be able to connect with our audience and there is the real possibility that the speech that we are giving will fail.

For more information on what it takes to be a great public speaker, check out my blog, The Accidental Communicator, at:

www.TheAccidentalCommunicator.com

Good luck!

- Dr. Jim Anderson

About The Author

I must confess that I never set out to be a public speaker. When I went to school, I studied Computer Science and thought that I'd get a nice job programming and that would be that. Well, at least part of that plan worked out!

My first job was working for Boeing on their F/A-18 fighter jet program. I spent my days programming fighter jet software in assembly language and I loved it. The U.S. government decided to save some money and went looking for other countries to sell this plane to. This put me into an unfamiliar role: I started to meet with foreign military officials and I ended up having to give speeches in order to explain what my product did.

Time moved on and so did I. I found myself working for Siemens, the big German telecommunications company. They were making phone switches and selling them to the seven U.S. phone companies. The problem was that the switches were too complicated. Customers couldn't tell the difference between one complicated phone switch from another complicated phone switch. Once again I found myself standing in front of the room giving speeches in order to explain what these complicated machines did and why ours were better than anyone else's.

I've spent over 25 years working as a product manager for both big companies and startups. This has given me an opportunity to do many, many presentations for customers, at conferences, and everywhere in-between.

I now live in Tampa Florida where I spend my time managing my consulting business, Blue Elephant Consulting, teaching college courses at the University of South Florida, and traveling to work with companies like yours to share the knowledge that I have about how to create and deliver powerful and effective speeches.

I'm always available to answer questions and I can be reached at:

Dr. Jim Anderson
Blue Elephant Consulting
Email: jim@BlueElephantConsulting.com
Facebook: http://goo.gl/1TVoK
Web: **www.BlueElephantConsulting.com**

"Unforgettable communication skills that will set your ideas free..."

Create Speeches That Motivate Your Audiences And Get Your Message Heard!

Dr. Jim Anderson is available to provide training and coaching on the topics that are the most important to people who have to speak in public: how can I create a speech that people want to hear and how can I deliver in a way that will allow me to connect with my audience and get my point across to them?

Dr. Anderson believes that in order to both learn and remember what he says, speakers need to laugh. Each one of his speeches is full of fun and humor so that what he says "sticks" with everyone.

Dr. Anderson's Public Speaking Training Includes:

1. How to plan your next speech: pick your purpose and understand your audience.
2. What's the best way to get PowerPoint and Keynote to work with you, not against you?
3. What do you need to do when you are presenting in order to truly connect with your audience?

Dr. Jim Anderson presents over 100 speeches per year. To invite Dr. Anderson to speak at your event, contact him at:

Phone: 813-418-6970 or
Email: jim@BlueElephantConsulting.com

Blue
Elephant
Consulting
Speaking   Negotiating   Managing   Marketing

13

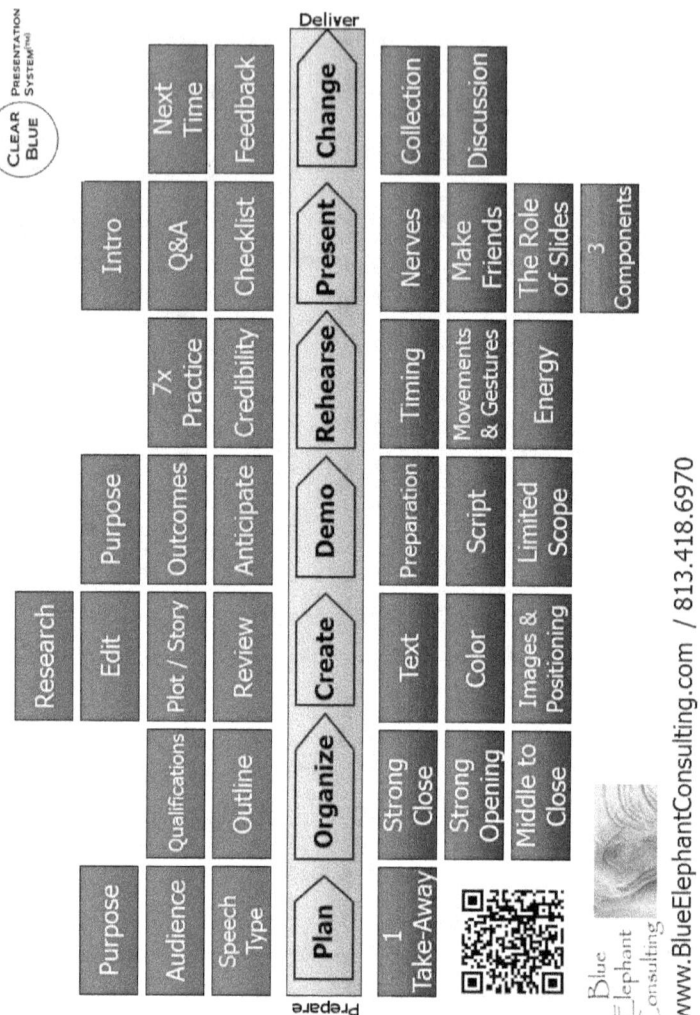

Blue Elephant Consulting has created the **Clear Blue™** presentation system for creating and delivering powerful and memorable presentations. The contents of this book are based on lessons learned during the development of the Clear Blue system. Contact Blue Elephant Consulting to learn more about the Clear Blue presentation system.

Chapter 1

Connect With Your Audience By Using Enthusiasm

Chapter 1: Connect With Your Audience By Using Enthusiasm

How many times have you gone to hear a speaker only to be disappointed? What was it that made you disappointed? I'm willing to bet that at least part of the problem was that **they were a boring speaker** – you didn't need to have great listening skills to discover that they didn't grab and hold your attention. Since you never want your audience to think about you in the same way, you've got to take steps to make sure that this never happens to you. It turn out that the solution to this speaking problem doesn't involve any presentation tips and is actually quite simple – get some enthusiasm!

Use Your Leadership Skills To Connect

It turns out that when we are speaking, we're not inhabiting someone else's body / life. It's really us up there. What this means is that we can bring all of other the skills that we have up there with us.

Leadership skills can be among the most important skills that a speaker can draw on during a presentation. The ability to stand tall, look your audience in the eyes, and tell them what you really want them to do **can go a long way in helping you to connect with your audience**. This is a great way to show the importance of public speaking.

Practice And Then Practice Again

Back in the day, practicing a speech meant that you had to sneak off to the bathroom and deliver your speech to yourself in the mirror. The mirror is still there waiting for you, but here in the 21st Century **we now have some additional tools** that will help you to get better before you have to give your next speech.

Just about any cell phone out there will allow you to **record your voice while you are talking**. I can't tell you the power of being able to sit back and play the role of an audience member listening to your speech. One of the key things that you'll be able to hear will be your energy level at different points in the speech. If it drops or rises at the wrong point, then go back and practice again!

Reach Out To Those Who Are Not Listening

When I'm working with first time speakers, one of the points that we go over is **the difference between a presentation and a report**. Unlike a report, when you are delivering a presentation you can sense your audience's level of interest in what you are saying. If it starts to wane, then you as the speaker need to take action.

There are a number of things that you can do to **shake things up**. Changing where you are physically at and moving into your audience can grab their attention. You can also start to ask questions of your audience and boost the overall energy of your speech. There's no way that they cannot pay attention to you now!

What All Of This Means For You

The reason that all of us go to the effort of getting up in front of an audience and go to the effort of delivering a speech is because **we want to make an impact on them**. We know the benefits of public speaking and we'll lose them if we come across as being boring because then this is not going to happen.

In order to make sure that we are able to connect with our audience, we need to **inject some enthusiasm into our next presentation**. This level of energy is infectious. If we can show our audience that we believe in what we are talking about, then what will happen is that we'll be able to draw them into our speech and get them excited.

Enthusiasm is not something that can be faked. As a speaker you are going to have to take a careful look at what you'll be talking about and find what part of it **captures your attention the most**. You can then use this part to generate the level of enthusiasm that you'll be able to use during your speech in order to make sure that you truly make an impact on your audience!

Chapter 2

Why Public Speakers Should Cut Out Filler Words

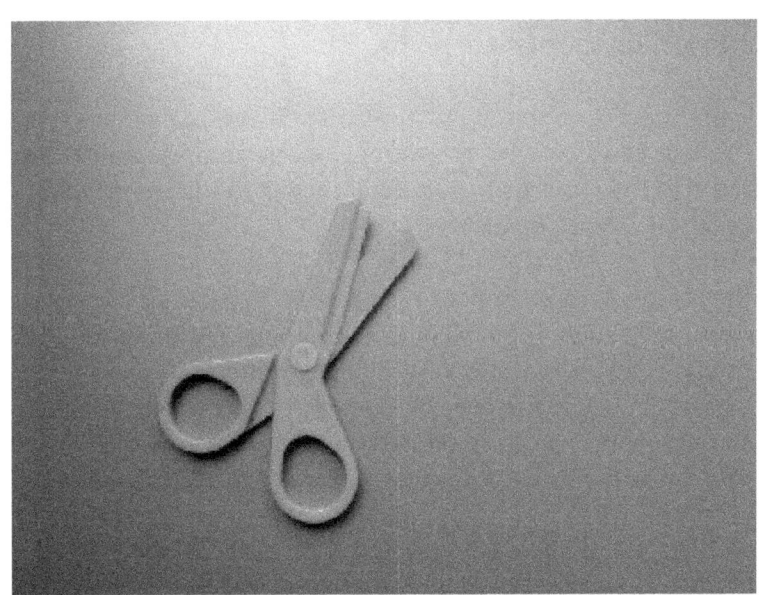

Chapter 2: Why Public Speakers Should Cut Out Filler Words

As we all strive to become better speakers, we tend to focus on **the big issues**: how to write a great speech, how to use our bodies to connect with our audience, etc. However, it turns out that sometimes it can be the little things that can trip us up. Things like using filler words in our speech.

Why Do We Use Filler Words?

Using filler words during a speech is a bad idea. The reasons that this is bad are actually pretty simple. Once your audience uses their listening skills and realizes that you are using words like "umm", "like", and "you know" in your speech then they will **become distracted** as they start to listen for the next time that you use one of these words.

If they start to do this, then they won't be able to hear anything else that you are saying no matter what clever presentation tips you use. The message that you were trying to share with your audience **will be completely lost**.

The reason that you or I might be using filler words is because **our brain is running so much faster than our mouth is**. As we go searching for the next thing that we want to say, our mouth runs out of words to say while the brain is off thinking up new ideas. Nobody likes to be silent during a speech so we "fill in" the gaps with filler words just to keep making noise. Never a good idea.

How Can We Stop Using Filler Words?

As speakers we want to find ways to stop using filler words. What this all comes down to is identifying ways that we can get our brain and our mouth to **operate at the same speed**.

One of the first things that we can do to reduce the number of filler words that we'll end up using during our next speech is to find ways to **boost our confidence** during our next speech. This can be as simple as reminding ourselves that our audience wants us to succeed. Realizing this make us less nervous and will reduce our need to add filler words to reduce the silence in our speech.

Often times we'll see speakers who are **not prepared to give a speech** use many filler words. The reason that they are doing this is because during their speech they can become distracted or uneasy and when this happens the filler words show up in force. Take the time to practice your next speech and this won't be a problem.

Finally, **you can't fix what you can't see**. Have a friend or a coworker listen to you deliver your speech. Show them what to look for and have them put their hand in the air every time you use a filler word. You'll be amazed at how often you are using filler words – at first. The nice thing about having a friend make you aware of this problem is how quickly it will go away once you have this awareness.

What Does All Of This Mean For You?

We all know about the importance of public speaking; however, even the best speakers can get tripped up if they use too many filler words. Filler words are unnecessary and they **distract our audience** from paying attention to the main message of our speech. As speakers, we need to find ways to eliminate filler words from our speeches so that our audiences can experience the benefits of public speaking.

There are a number of ways to go about doing this. The first and the simplest is to **become confidant** about what you are talking about. The next is to take the time to practice your speech enough – in this case practice does make perfect. Finally, you need a friend who will listen to your speech and give your feedback on your use of filler words.

The good news about filler words is that once we become aware that we're using them, **they'll go away quickly**. Take the time to work on eliminating them from your next speech and you'll be amazed at how much more of an effective speaker you will become!

Chapter 3

Good Public Speakers Are Really Good Models

Chapter 3: Good Public Speakers Are Really Good Models

In order to become a better public speaker than you are right now, just exactly what do you have to do? If you are like most of us, you probably said "become more like…" and named a famous public speaker that you admire. Well guess what, that person is going to **help you to reach the next level** in your public speaking ability…

Why Modeling Works

Just to be clear about what we're going to be talking about here: it's not about how you can make it to the catwalks of Paris or London. Rather, we're going to be talking about how your next speech can start to **look like it was being given by a public speaker that you admire**.

Modeling is really about having you **draw inspiration** from someone that you believe does a good job of speaking in public. It could be Suzy Orman, Tony Robbins, or even the late Steve Jobs. Wanting to be able to speak like one of these famous speakers is a perfectly natural desire. We all understand the importance of public speaking, now we just want to get good at it.

The key is to understand why we want to go to the effort to model them. We don't really want to be them, rather what we want to be able to do is to **get the same results from an audience that they do**. We want our audiences to laugh, cry, and get motivated to do what we are asking them to do. The ability to make that happen is where the real power of modeling comes through.

How To Model A Public Speaker

If I've been able to convince you that modeling a speaker that you admire is a good thing to do, now comes the hard part: **how to do it?** It turns out that there are only three areas that you need to focus your modeling on.

1. **Presence:** How we stand and how we move while giving a speech is an important part of who we are. When you want to model a speaker, you need to take the time to study their on-stage physical presence. How do they enter the stage: do they stride in and take it over or do they start in the background and move forward? Do they stay in one place or do they move around a lot? Watch and learn.

2. **Voice:** As speakers we don't have a lot of tools with which to deliver a speech. However, our voice is something that either helps us or hurts us when we are giving our next speech. Watch how the speaker that you want to emulate uses his or her voice. Things that should stand out include how loud they are and if they vary their sound levels. How fast they talk and if they change their pace during a speech. Finally, listen to see if they speak in a higher or lower tone during their speech to indicate excitement.

3. **Words:** Ultimately, the goal of any speech is to paint a mental picture in your audience's head. You want them to be able to "see" what you are talking about. How does the speaker that you want to be like accomplish this task? Do they use lots of big words or do they use common everyday words that we are all familiar with. How good of a mental picture do they paint?

What All Of This Means For You

In order to move from where you are in your public speaking skills **to the next level**, you need to identify a public speaker that you admire and would like to emulate. Then you need to model them. The ability to constantly be working to become a better public speaker is one of the benefits of public speaking.

Modeling works because as we pretend to be someone, **our skills and techniques develop** and we actually start to take on some of the skills that that person has. Taking the time to copy a speaker's physical presence, their voice and their words will allow you to "become them".

If we don't change, then we risk remaining the same forever. Take the time to find a speaker that is the speaker that you would like to become. Study them and then the next time that you give a speech model their best qualities. By doing this you'll be able to first pretend to be a better speaker and then **become the speaker that you want to be**.

Chapter 4

Acting Lessons Help Us To Become Better Public Speakers

Chapter 4: Acting Lessons Help Us To Become Better Public Speakers

As public speakers, it can be very easy for us to become nervous or upset about our next speech despite our understanding of the importance of public speaking. This can happen at any time, even to experienced speakers. The big question is **what can we do about it?** It turns out that one solution has been used by actors and actresses to solve this very same problem.

Play The Role Of The Speaker That You Would Like To Be

In order to deal with an attack of the nerves, you need to find ways to **boost your self-confidence**. One way to go about doing this is to try to find out just exactly why you have become nervous. More often than not you'll discover that you have become afraid of doing something wrong – making a mistake while you are giving a speech.

In order to overcome this problem, what actors do is they identify someone that they respect and admire, another actor, whom they believe could play a given role perfectly. When they've identified this person, they then **"play" that person** and start to imitate them when they are performing.

This is exactly what you and I can do when we find that we have suddenly become nervous about our next speaking opportunity. It doesn't take much to picture a world famous speaker, perhaps Tony Robbins, delivering the speech that we've been asked to give. When we can see this being done in our mind's eye, then it becomes easy for us to **"play" them** when we are on stage and do a great job.

Create Your Own Green Room

In the world of acting, actors never just show up and go on stage. Instead, there is a warm-up period that they go through in order to become ready to take the stage. This warm-up happens offstage and is generally done in what is called **the "green room"**.

In the green room an actor is **removed from the audience** that he or she will be performing for. This gives them an opportunity to warm up their voice, visualize the performance that they'll be delivering, etc. The challenge that we have as speakers is that unless you are speaking at a very large event, you won't have access to a green room before your next speech.

What this means for you is that you are going to have to **create your own "green room"**. This means that you'll need to start to show up for your speaking engagements early. By doing this you'll be able to find quiet places before your presentation that you can use as your very own green room. Note that every speaking location will have a bathroom and in a pinch, this is where you can get the quiet time that you'll need to get ready.

What All Of This Means For You

An **attack of the nerves** can hit any speaker no matter how much experience they have. In order to make sure that this does not derail the next speech that you've been asked to deliver or take away from the benefits of public speaking for your audience, you need to take a lesson from the world of professional actors and actresses.

In order to do the thing that makes you nervous, don't do it as yourself. Instead, **play the role of a speaker that you admire** and "become" them while you are giving your speech. Also make sure that you create your own "green room" by arriving early to give your speech so that you can warm up.

As difficult and challenging as many of our speeches are, actors and actresses have been **dealing with the same issues of stage fright for as long as we have**. Learn from the techniques that they've developed to deal with these stressful situations and you'll become a better public speaker.

Chapter 5

Creating High Quality "A's" For Q&As

Chapter 5: Creating High Quality "A's" For Q&As

As public speakers, we understand the importance of public speaking and so we take the time to prepare our speeches. We clearly identify who we'll be talking to, pick a topic, build a speech, practice it, and then deliver it. That's all there is to this public speaking stuff, right? Well, not exactly. There's the little thing called **the "Q&A" portion of the speech** where your audience can ask you questions about what you just said (or anything else that they want to). Got a plan for handling this?

Getting Ready To Answer A Question

There you stand, worn out from delivering the best speech of your life and now a member of your audience has asked you a tricky question. **What is a speaker to do?** Don't worry about this, it's important that you view answering your audience's questions as being easier to do than giving a speech – you can do this!

What you're going to want to do as you prepare to provide the audience with an answer to the question that has been asked is to **buy yourself some time**. The easiest way to go about doing this is by simply repeating aloud the question that you've been asked. This will actually accomplish two things at the same time.

The first is that it will, of course, buy you time and allow you to process in your mind just exactly what the question is – it always helps if we can hear something several times before we have to answer it. Next, by repeating the question back to the person who asked it you are able to **confirm that you'll be answering the right question** – did you hear what they asked correctly?

The Body Of Your Answer

The body of your answer is where most of the information is going to go. What you're going to want to do here is to start out by laying out your thesis – **the main point in your response**.

Your next step is going to be to back this thesis up with some supporting material. Since you are thinking on your feet and don't have a lot of time here, you're going to want to **limit your justification to only three points**.

If it turns out that three points are too much for you to come up with, feel free to only provide two justification points for your thesis. However, try to stay away from **just providing one justification point** because this probably won't satisfy the person who is asking the question.

Wrapping It All Up

As you start to wrap up your answer to the question that you've been asked, you're going to want to once again **revisit what you've already said**. In your conclusion you're going to want to restate your main point and the justification points that you used to back it up.

You may want to add one more thing to your answer. As you wrap it up, you could choose to **touch on any challenges** that may be brought up against your answer. By briefly discussing them as a part of your answer, you can defuse them before anyone gets a chance to ask you another question about your answer.

What All Of This Means For You

Creating and delivering a speech is a big task. However, it turns out that there's often more to public speaking than just that. All too often speeches come equipped with **a "Q&A" period** right after you get done giving your speech where your audience gets a chance to ask you questions. You had better be ready for this.

You need to view the answers that you give to your audience's questions **as being mini-speeches**. Each of these mini-speeches will have an opening, a body, and a closing. You'll be thinking on your feet so be sure to use every technique to buy yourself time to think.

Your audience will leave your speech with the last words out of your mouth ringing in their heads. What this means for you is that there is a good chance that how your answer their questions is the thing that they'll remember after your speech is over. You need to come prepared to **deliver great answers to whatever questions they ask**. Get good at doing this and one of the benefits of public speaking is that you'll be the speaker who always gets asked to come back!

Chapter 6

Hey Public Speaker, Do You Want To Debate?

Chapter 6: Hey Public Speaker, Do You Want To Debate?

Not all speeches are equal. In fact, some speeches are much more dynamic and aggressive than others. One great example of this is a debate. A debate is a great way to show the importance of public speaking. In a debate, you can prepare for the discussion, but you can't completely prepare for it. Instead, **you're going to have to think on your feet.** As you might well imagine, this style of speaking can get to be quite tricky very quickly…

Four Ways To Prepare For A Debate

When you know that you are going to be involved in a debate, you need to show up ready. As speakers, we all know about creating a speech and practicing it. A debate is a bit different – yes, there will be some speaking to be done, but **it's going to be a lot more dynamic.** In order to be an effective speaker at your next debate, here are four ways that you can prepare to be successful:

1. Pick A Position: Every debate is about something. No matter if you are running for a chair on the city council or if you are going to be talking about which science book should be used in the local schools, you need to have a position going into the debate. When you show up for the debate, you are going to want to make sure that you have brought along evidence to support your position – because the other side will have done this!

2. Be Ready For Counterarguments: It is the very nature of a debate for the other side of the debate to push back against whatever position you are taking. What this means for you is that long before the debate occurs, you need to take the time and think about what their counterarguments may be and how best to respond to them.

3. Own The Lectern: So much of a debate has to do with the level of self-confidence that you project to the audience. In order to come across as though you know what you are talking about, you need to own the lectern. This means that when you take the stage you stride to the lectern and you make it yours. You don't come across as being timid or weak – let everyone know that you are right where you need to be.

4. Rise To The Scrutiny: What you say during a debate will be questioned by the other party. They may pick it apart and they may come back at you with questions based on what you've said. You need to anticipate this happening and you need to keep your cool. They are not attacking you personally, but rather trying to sell their ideas by discounting yours. You need to rise to the occasion and address their questions in a cool and confident manner.

What All Of This Means For You

A very important form of speaking is the debate. This style of speaking uses the benefits of public speaking to allow your audience to hear two sides of an issue or see how two (or more) different candidates would deal with an important issue. Debating is not easy to do, but **it is a very important skill to have**.

In order to prepare for a debate, you need to make sure that **you have a position on a topic** and that you know why you have it. You also have to take the time to anticipate how your debate partner is going to counter your position. While you are speaking you need to make sure that you command the lectern Finally, take the time to learn how to remain cool during a debate.

The good news is that a debate is **a very powerful form of communication**. The bad news is that it is conducted in an adversarial environment and it can be very hard to do correctly. Take the time to follow the four suggestions that we've reviewed and the next time that you're asked to participate in a debate, you'll be ready!

Chapter 7

Public Speakers Need To Know How To Master Time

Chapter 7: Public Speakers Need To Know How To Master Time

Time is a funny thing. Before we start to deliver a speech, it can seem as though we have all of the time in the world – how ever are we going to fill up the time that we've been given to deliver our speech in? However, once we take the stage or step into the front of the room, time seems to speed up and there never seems to be enough of it. In order to maximize the importance of public speaking, **how can we become better at managing this time thing?**

Practice, Practice, Practice

In order to get control over your time, the very first step that you need to take is **to time how long it takes you to deliver your speech when you are practicing it**. It should be pretty clear that if you can't complete your speech in the allotted time during a practice run, then you're not going to be able to do so when you give your speech for real.

However, something that a lot of us don't realize is that the real world of giving speeches is a lot different from the quiet world in which we practice our speeches. What this means is that even if your speech does fit into the allotted time in practice, when you account for audience laughter, questions, and unplanned interruptions **your speech may still be too long.**

It's All About The Handout

When you give a speech, you have important information that you want to share with your audience. There is always a possibility that **you may not be able to cover everything that you want to in your speech**. That's why it makes sense to provide your audience with a handout that contains a summary of all of your important points.

Note that when I say handout I do not mean a copy of the slides that you may have presented. Instead, **it should be additional information** that will allow you to focus on the most important details in your speech. Additionally, if your time gets cut short, you can always refer your audience to your handout.

Buy Yourself More Time – Arrive Early

No matter how well you work to make sure that your speech will fit into the amount of time that you've been given, **things can always happen**. What this means for you is that you need to always be sure to arrive early whenever you are going to be giving a speech.

The reasons for doing this are many and varied. You are going to want to make sure that the room where you'll be speaking has been set up properly. You are also going to want to test out all of the necessary equipment to make sure that it works before you start your speech. Get these things taken care of before you start to speak and **you'll make sure that they don't cut into your speaking time**.

What All Of This Means For You

As much time as we spend trying to get our words right for our next speech, it turns out that there is something that may be even more important: **time**. We never have an unlimited amount of time to deliver a speech and it's up to us to maximize the benefits of public speaking by making the most of the time that we've been given.

It all starts with practice. We need to make sure that we can deliver our speech within the time that we've been allocated.

We need to make sure that we've allotted for audience induced delays. Next we need to provider our audience with a handout. This will cover any gaps if we have to shorten our speech to meet the available time. Finally, every time you are asked to deliver a speech, make sure that you show up early. This will allow you to resolve any issues without having to waste time during your speech solving problems.

The one thing that there never seems to be enough of is time. As public speakers **we need to respect the fact that we don't control our time**; however, we need to take the time to do everything that we possibly can to make the most of the time that we have been given...

Chapter 8

---

3 Reasons Why Speakers Fail

Chapter 8: 3 Reasons Why Speakers Fail

Every time we stand in front of an audience, we are filled with the hope that we are **going to be able to connect with our audience** and get our message across to them – this is what the , importance of public speaking is all about. However, this does not always happen. When it doesn't happen, we need to take a step back and take the time to understand what happened. It turns out that more often than not, there are three reasons why we may fail to connect with an audience.

When Your Audience Does Not Relate To You

In order to connect with our audience, we need to be able get them to relate to us. It turns out that this may be harder to do than you think. One of the reasons that it can be a real challenge is because we tend to include in our speeches **stories about our successes** – the challenges that we've faced and how we've overcome them. If we are not careful, our audience will hear what we are saying and decide "I could never do that" and then they'll shut out anything else that we have to say.

When Your Audience Is Not Sold On Your Message

If you don't take the time to prepare your audience for your speech, then you are going to be dealing with the dreaded "cold room" – an audience that is really **not sure why they are sitting there** or what you are going to be talking about. Your audience has to know how they are going to benefit from your speech or you'll never be able to connect with them. If you do this right, long before you take the stage your audience will be excited to hear what you have to say.

When Your Audience Is Not Motivated To Take The Next Step

So why are you even bothering to give this speech? I suspect it is because **you are trying to motivate your audience to take some sort of action**. This can be to lose some weight, vote a certain way, or buy your product. If you don't do a good job of selling them on the results that they are going to be able to achieve by taking a specific set of actions after your speech is over, then you won't be able to connect with them and they'll end up doing nothing as a result of listening to your speech.

What All Of This Means For You

Giving a speech is hard work. We're willing to go to the effort of creating and delivering a speech because we believe in the benefits of public speaking and that **we can make a difference** in the lives of the members of our audience. However, all too often we fail to do this. When this happens, we need to take the time to understand what happened.

There are many reasons **why a speaker may fail to connect with his or her audience**. One reason is because your audience didn't relate to you. You just seemed to be too different. Another reason is because the message that you were delivering needs to relate to your audience. If they don't understand how they will benefit from what you are saying, they won't care. Finally, your audience may end up being unwilling to take the next step. If the benefits that you laid out were not compelling enough, then they won't bother.

Knowing how you can fail as a speaker is critical information. Once you know this, **you then know what you need to avoid**. There is no guarantee that you'll be able to connect with your audience during every speech that you give. However, if you know what not to do, you've just boosted your chances of success!

Chapter 9

Mistakes That We Speakers Make

Chapter 9: Mistakes That We Speakers Make

I'm pleased to be able to announce that I understand the importance of public speaking and **I am a perfect speaker**. I never make a mistake. Ok, well, I guess that I do make mistakes sometimes. Well, I guess that I really make a lot of mistakes. Ok, so I guess I'm not a perfect speaker. However, I'm willing to bet that you are not a perfect speaker either. In order for us non-perfect speakers to become better, we need to take a look at what we are doing and see if we can spot the mistakes that we are making. If we can do this, then perhaps we can become just a little bit more perfect each time we give a speech!

You Are Asking Your Audience To Do Too Much

One error that we speakers tend to make is that for some odd reason **we decide to ask our audience to do too much**. The reason that we are giving a speech more often than not is because we want our audience to do something. Where things can go wrong is when we ask them to do a number of different things. This can easily confuse our audience (what was I supposed to do first?) and when that happens the old phrase "a confused mind says no" comes into play. Instead of confusing our audiences, we need to limit what we are asking them to do to one single thing.

Your Audience Does Not Feel Involved In Your Speech

Your speech is something that you have created and you are sharing with your audience. It can be very easy for us to make the error of **not creating a speech that our audience can connect with**. What we need to do as speakers is to find ways to take the speech that we've created by ourselves and turn it into a speech that our audience feels that they have had a hand in creating.

There are a lot of different ways to go about making this happen. One is to **take the time to ask your audience questions** while you are delivering your speech. Another is to use topical references to things that have gone on during the day that you are making your presentation. Additionally, involving your audience in your stories will also draw them into your speech and make them feel like it is really their speech instead of just yours.

Your Audience Knows That This Is Not Your First Time

Let's face it, we often get asked to give the same speech to multiple audiences. When we are asked to do this, something very dangerous can occur. Our audience figures out that **this is not our first time for giving this speech**. They realize that they are listening to a "canned" speech and so they start to tune us out.

What we need to do as speakers in order to prevent making this error, is to **find ways to "freshen up" every speech that we give**. Yes, the majority of the speech may be a speech that we've given before; however, that doesn't mean that we can't change things up. We can add a new story, we can add a new line or do something that makes this telling of our speech different from all of the other times that we've given it. Additionally, it can help to picture a person that you are going to be giving this speech for. Knowing that there is one person that you are doing this for can help you to keep your focus and understand that what you are doing is important.

What All Of This Means For You

No speaker, including me, is ever perfect. It can be all too easy for us to **make simple mistakes** when we are delivering a speech and thereby diminish the benefits of public speaking. The secret to becoming a better speaker is to understand the types of mistakes that we may be making, realize when we are making them, and then take steps to correct ourselves.

There are **many different types of errors** that speakers can make. One is when we ask our audiences to take too many steps after our speech is over. We need to limit the things that we ask our audience to do to just one thing. Next, if we don't find a way to get our audience to feel as though they are involved in our speech, then we won't be able to make an impact on them. Finally, although we may have given this speech before, we need to find ways to "freshen it up" and make our audience feel as though this is the first time that we've given this speech.

It's no fun when we screw things up by making errors when we are giving a speech. However, the good news is that **all of the errors that we may make can be easily spotted and corrected**. Take the time to make sure that the three errors that we've discussed are not a part of your next speech!

Chapter 10

Basic Mistakes That Speakers Make

Chapter 10: Basic Mistakes That Speakers Make

As speakers, **we are always trying to get better at what we do** because we know about the importance of public speaking. We may learn to do new things with our voice, our body, or the way that we tell stories during our speeches. However, on top of learning to do all of these new things, we also have to unlearn the mistakes that we may be making right now. The first step in doing this is to become aware of some of the more common mistakes that speakers make.

Not Totally Showing Up For Your Speech

Our goal during every speech that we give is to find a way to **connect with our audience**. Under the best of circumstances, this can be a tough thing to do. However, if during our speech we are not emotionally invested in the stories that we are telling or we just are not "all there", then there is no way that we're going to be able to connect with our audience. The end result of this is that we'll end up giving a speech that does not have an impact on our audience and we won't be able to change the world.

Failing To Do Your Research

In order to convince our audience to change the world, we're going to need to be able to **convince them to take action**. If we want to have any hope of doing this, we're going to have to be able to present a logical set of reasons why they should change. This kind of logic is going to require that we share both facts and stats with our audience. What this means for us is that we've got some homework to do before we deliver our next speech. If we fail to do the research that is required in order to uncover the facts that will sway our audience, then once again we'll miss an opportunity to change our audience's minds.

Causing An Energy Mismatch

Most of us don't spend a lot of time thinking about what our audience's energy level is when we take the stage to deliver a speech. However, it turns out that this is very, very important. When we start a speech, we need to **match our audience's current energy level**. This allows us to get their attention. If we start out too low or too high, then we won't connect with them and they'll start to ignore what we are saying. By taking the time to understand their energy level and matching it, we can connect with them at the start of our speech and get them to come along with us during the rest of our speech.

What All Of This Means For You

The goal of every speaker is to **become a better speaker** every time that we give a speech so that we can share the benefits of public speaking. It is all too easy for us to make a mistake; however, the most important thing is for us to realize when we make a mistake and to not repeat it.

Classic speaker mistakes include **not mentally showing up for a speech**. There are a lot of things that can distract us and if we're not careful our audience will be able to tell when our mind is somewhere else. Every speech needs us to have our facts and stats correct. If we don't take the time to do our research, our audience who are probably experts on the topic that we are talking about will quickly catch on to the fact that we don't know what we are talking about. Finally, our audience will either be excited to hear what we have to say or not. As a speaker we need to make an effort to match their energy level so that we bring them along with us.

The good news about all three of these basic speaker mistakes is that they are easy to spot when they occur and easy to fix. Make sure that you are aware of the mistakes that you can make so that you'll have your eyes open. We may not have the ability to turn you into a perfect speaker, but at least we can **reduce the number of basic mistakes you'll make!**

Chapter 11

All The World's A Stage – You Just Have To Know How To Use It

Chapter 11: All The World's A Stage – You Just Have To Know How To Use It

When we give a speech we may not always be on a stage. However, we always have a space that has been given to us to use as our own during the speech. All too often we see speakers doing things that they should not be doing – pacing, circling, hanging out in one corner or another. A stage (or speaking area) is a fantastic tool for speakers that helps to boost the importance of public speaking, **but how are we supposed to use it?**

As A Way To Show Action

For someone who does a lot of talking, **there sure seems to be a lot of action in my speeches**. I find myself telling stories in which people do thing, objects move around, etc. It's great when I tell my audience about all of this motion, but when I'm on stage, it's even better if I show them.

When I'm telling a story in which a character moves around, I need to make those movements on my stage **so that my audience can "see" what's going on in my story**. I can also create a virtual object like a door and open it and go through it if it will help make my story clearer.

One important thing to realize about showing action while you are up on stage is that **not all actions are created the same**. What this means is that depending on how your story is going, your actions can be delivered either fast or slow. You need to match what you are doing on the stage with what is going on in your speech.

As A Way To Create A Speech Timeline

Many of the speeches that we give **deal with the tricky issue of time**. The challenge that we face as speakers is that although we may move through a considerable amount of time in our speech, we may not be able to bring our audience along with us if they don't realize that time is passing.

This is where your stage can come into play. What you are going to want to do is to stand in one position while you share with your audience what happened at a given point in time. Then, as time moves on, **you'll want to move to another spot on the stage** in order to visually show your audience that time has advanced.

If you are speaking in the western world, **your audience will read from left to right**. What this means for you as a speaker is that you are going to want to start your time-based movement on your stage from your left to your right. This will match with how your audience thinks that you should move through time.

As A Way To Structure Our Stage

Some of our speeches **don't actually have a clear sequence of events to them**. Yes, we've got a lot of information that we want to share with our audience, but each one of the items that we want to share basically stands by itself. You can use the stage to help communicate information like this also.

What you are going to want to do is to want to associate different spots on the stage **with different ideas that you want to cover in your speech**. As you complete an idea that you want to share with your audience, you will want to physically move to a different spot on the stage.

The power of this technique is that it allows you to **show the sequence of ideas** that make up your speech. You'll want to be careful to pick a good place on stage to start your speech and a meaningful spot to wrap things up.

What All Of This Means For You

It can be rather lonely up there on stage – really it's only you and your words. However, it turns out that you really have something else to help you to **deliver a powerful and effective speech**: the stage. Now all you have to do is to figure out how to use it correctly to maximize the benefits of public speaking.

If the speech that you are giving has action in it, either something that you did or something that a character that you are talking about did, then **use your stage to show your audience that action is happening**. If what you are talking about happens over time, then start at one place on the stage and move side-to-side to show your audience that time is progressing. Finally, if your speech has multiple parts to it, then you can assign a part to a place on the stage and move from spot to spot as you move through your speech.

All too often we overlook the power of the stage when we are giving a speech. Many speakers take the center of the stage and spend their entire speech just standing there. Don't do this! Instead, **plan out how you can use your stage** to provide your speech with both variety and impact.

Chapter 12

Learn To Speak Like Your Audience

Chapter 12: Learn To Speak Like Your Audience

You can attend all of the fancy speaking classes that you want, but there is a very good chance that they are not going to teach you what you really need to know. The reason that they won't is because despite the importance of public speaking, they don't know what you are really looking for. However, I do. What you want most as a public speaker is **for your next audience to fall in love with you**. To treasure your every word. To not only understand what you are saying, but also to come to believe what you are saying. In order to make this happen, you need to become more like your audience.

Learn How To Listen

So who does your audience really want to spend their time listening to? Well, if we're going to be honest about this, **they'd prefer to listen to themselves**. What this means for you is that you need to spend the time to make yourself become more like them.

The way that this starts is by having you take the time to become a good listener. **You need to listen to your audience**. How do they speak? What words do they use? Do they speak fast or slow? Knowing that they really want to listen to themselves, we need to listen and adapt how we speak so that we start to speak more like they do.

Imitation Is The Greatest Form Of Flattery

In order to become more like your audience, you are going to have to **practice becoming more like them**. The way that you can go about doing this is to record what they sound like. There are a number of different ways that you can go about capturing them talking on tape, but make sure that you do it because it will be well worth the effort.

Once you have a recording of how the members of your next audience talk, take the time to listen to it. As you listen, stop the recording and **practice talking like they do**. No, you'll never be mistaken as a native, but perhaps you can get close before it's time for you to deliver your speech.

You Can't Exaggerate Enough

In order to express yourself more like your audience does, you are going to have to **practice communicating like they do**. You are going to want to go "all in" here. This means that as you practice you do it in a big way.

A big way means that you make all of your sounds big – bigger than they need to be in real life. Yes, I do realize how ridiculous this may all seem to you, but it is important. You need to **go "over the top"** when you start to practice communicating like your audience does. As you get better at doing this, you can tone it down.

No Reason To Be Shy

Your audience is going to know that you are different from them. When you start to communicate with them using the words, tones, and mannerisms that they use they are not going to know what to think. **This opens an opportunity for you.**

You can use their surprise to play with how you communicate with them. Feel free to **do some experimentation here**. The more you become like them, the more surprised they will be. Have fun with your audience. You've worked hard to connect with them so make the most of the moment.

What All Of This Means For You

In this big world of ours, it turns out that every public speaker wants to be able to accomplish the same thing: **we want to make our next audience love us**. To make this happen and to realize all of the benefits of public speaking, all we have to do is one thing: become more like they are.

This may sound simple, but it turns out that **it's actually quite difficult to do correctly**. The first thing that you need to do is to teach yourself how to listen to your audience so that you can pick up on the unique aspects that make up how they communicate with each other. Once you know how they do it, imitate it and then exaggerate how you do it when you start to practice it. Finally, don't be shy – play with your audience as you communicate with them in a way that they want.

Becoming your audience is the key to successfully connecting with them. In order to do this requires you to **do some homework** and learn how your audience likes to be communicated with. Take the time to do this correctly and you will have discovered how to speak like your audience...

It's from the forge of failure that the steel of success is formed.

Hard Work Does Not Guarantee Success, But Success Does Not Happen Without Hard Work.

- Dr. Jim Anderson

Create Speeches That Motivate Your Audiences And Get Your Message Heard!

Dr. Jim Anderson is available to provide training and coaching on the topics that are the most important to people who have to speak in public: how can I create a speech that people want to hear and how can I deliver in a way that will allow me to connect with my audience and get my point across to them?

Dr. Anderson believes that in order to both learn and remember what he says, speakers need to laugh. Each one of his speeches is full of fun and humor so that what he says "sticks" with everyone.

Dr. Anderson's Public Speaking Training Includes:

1. How to plan your next speech: pick your purpose and understand your audience.
2. What's the best way to get PowerPoint and Keynote to work with you, not against you?
3. What do you need to do when you are presenting in order to truly connect with your audience?

Dr. Jim Anderson presents over 100 speeches per year. To invite Dr. Anderson to speak at your event, contact him at:

Phone: 813-418-6970 or
Email: jim@BlueElephantConsulting.com

Blue
Elephant
Consulting

Speaking   Negotiating   Managing   Marketing

Photo Credits:

Cover - U.S. Pacific Command

https://www.flickr.com/photos/us-pacific-command/

Chapter 1 - Lamya Rashid

https://www.flickr.com/photos/karroozi/

Chapter 2 - John Cooper

https://www.flickr.com/photos/atomicshed/

Chapter 3 - Automotive Rhythms

https://www.flickr.com/photos/artvlive/

Chapter 4 - Kevin Dooley

https://www.flickr.com/photos/pagedooley/

Chapter 5 - Benjamin Reay

https://www.flickr.com/photos/benjreay/

Chapter 6 - Gina Parody

https://www.flickr.com/photos/ginaparody/

Chapter 7 - Michelle Ramos

https://www.flickr.com/photos/michelleramos/

Chapter 8 - Chris Griffith

https://www.flickr.com/photos/chrisgriffith/

Chapter 9 – sisssou

https://www.flickr.com/photos/sissou/

Chapter 10 - Lisa Moffatt

https://www.flickr.com/photos/72427965@N00/

Chapter 11 - Chris Smart

https://www.flickr.com/photos/sigma/

Chapter 12 – Indabelle

https://www.flickr.com/photos/indabelle/

Other Books By The Author

Product Management

- Manage Your Customers, Manage Your Product: Techniques For Product Managers To Better Understand What Their Customers Really Want

- How Product Managers Can Sell More Of Their Product: Tips & Techniques For Product Managers To Better Understand How To Sell Their Product

- How Product Managers Can Sell More Of Their Product: Tips & Techniques For Product Managers To Better Understand How To Sell Their Product

- How To Create A Successful Product That Customers Will Want: Techniques For Product Managers To Boost Product Sales And Increase Customer Satisfaction

- What Product Managers Need To Know About World-Class Product Development: How Product Managers Can Create Successful Products

- How Product Managers Can Learn To Understand Their Customers: Techniques For Product

Managers To Better Understand What Their
Customers Really Want

- Product Management Secrets: Techniques For
  Product Managers To Boost Product Sales And
  Increase Customer Satisfaction

- Product Development Lessons For Product
  Managers: How Product Managers Can Create
  Successful Products

- Customer Lessons For Product Managers:
  Techniques For Product Managers To Better
  Understand What Their Customers Really Want

- Product Failure Lessons For Product Managers:
  Examples Of Products That Have Failed For Product
  Managers To Learn From

- Communication Skills For Product Managers: The
  Communication Skills That Product Managers Need
  To Know How To Use In Order To Have A Successful
  Product

- How To Have A Successful Product Manager
  Career: The Things That You Need To Be Doing
  TODAY In Order To Have A Successful Product
  Manager Career

- Product Manager Product Success: How to keep your product on track and make it become a success

Public Speaking

- Creating Speeches That Work: How To Create A Speech That Will Make Your Message Be Remembered Forever!

- How To Organize A Speech In Order To Make Your Point: How to put together a speech that will capture and hold your audience's attention

- Changing How You Speak To Overcome Your Fear Of Speaking: Change techniques that will transform a speech into a memorable event

- Delivering Excellence: How To Give Presentations That Make A Difference: Presentation techniques that will transform a speech into a memorable event

- Tools Speakers Need In Order To Give The Perfect Speech: What tools to use to create your next speech so that your message will be remembered forever!

- How To Create A Speech That Will Be Remembered

- Secrets To Organizing A Speech For Maximum Impact: How to put together a speech that will capture and hold your audience's attention

- How To Become A Better Speaker By Changing How You Speak: Change techniques that will transform a speech into a memorable event

- How To Give A Great Presentation: Presentation techniques that will transform a speech into a memorable event

- How To Rehearse In Order To Give The Perfect Speech: How to effectively rehearse your next speech to that your message be remembered forever!

- Secrets To Creating The Perfect Speech: How to create a speech that will make your message be remembered forever!

- Secrets To Organizing The Perfect Speech: How to organize the best speech of your life!

- Secrets To Planning The Perfect Speech: How to plan to give the best speech of your life

- How To Show What You Mean During A Presentation: How to use visual techniques to transform a speech into a memorable event

CIO Skills

- How CIOs Can Bring Business And IT Together: How CIOs Can Use Their Technical Skills To Help Their Company Solve Real-World Business Problems

- New IT Technology Issues Facing CIOs: How CIOs Can Stay On Top Of The Changes In The Technology That Powers The Company

- Keeping The Barbarians Out: How CIOs Can Secure Their Department and Company: Tips And Techniques For CIOs To Use In Order To Secure Both Their IT Department And Their Company

- What CIOs Need To Know In Order To Successfully Manage An IT Department: Decision Making Skills That Every CIO Needs To Have In Order To Be Able To Make The Right Choices

- Becoming A Powerful And Effective Leader: Tips And Techniques That IT Managers Can Use In Order To Develop Leadership Skills

- CIO Secrets For Growing Innovation: Tips And Techniques For CIOs To Use In Order To Make Innovation Happen In Their IT Department

- Your Success As A CIO Depends On How Well You Communicate: Tips And Techniques For CIOs To Use In Order To Become Better Communicators

- What CIOs Need To Know About Working With Partners: Techniques For CIOs To Use In Order To Be Able To Successfully Work With Partners

- Critical CIO Management Skills: Decision Making Skills That Every CIO Needs To Have In Order To Be Able To Make The Right Choices

- How CIOs Can Make Innovation Happen: Tips And Techniques For CIOs To Use In Order To Make Innovation Happen In Their IT Department

- CIO Communication Skills Secrets: Tips And Techniques For CIOs To Use In Order To Become Better Communicators

- Managing Your CIO Career: Steps That CIOs Have To Take In Order To Have A Long And Successful Career

- CIO Business Skills: How CIOs can work effectively with the rest of the company!

IT Manager Skills

- How IT Managers Can Use New Technology To Meet Today's IT Challenges: Technologies That IT Managers Can Use In Order to Make Their Teams More Productive

- How To Build High Performance IT Teams: Tips And Techniques That IT Managers Can Use In Order To Develop Productive Teams

- Save Yourself, Save Your Job – How To Manage Your IT Career: Secrets That IT Managers Can Use In Order To Have A Successful Career

- Growing Your CIO Career: How CIOs Can Work With The Entire Company In Order To Be Successful

- How IT Managers Can Make Innovation Happen: Tips And Techniques For IT Managers To Use In Order To Make Innovation Happen In Their Teams

- Staffing Skills IT Managers Must Have: Tips And Techniques That IT Managers Can Use In Order To Correctly Staff Their Teams

- Secrets Of Effective Leadership For IT Managers: Tips And Techniques That IT Managers Can Use In Order To Develop Leadership Skills

- IT Manager Career Secrets: Tips And Techniques That IT Managers Can Use In Order To Have A Successful Career

- IT Manager Budgeting Skills: How IT Managers Can Request, Manage, Use, And Track Their Funding

- Secrets Of Managing Budgets: What IT Managers Need To Know In Order To Understand How Their Company Uses Money

Negotiating

- The Art Of Packaging A Negotiation: How To Develop The Skill Of Assembling Potential Trades In Order To Get The Best Possible Outcome

- Getting What You Want In A Negotiation By Learning How To Signal: How To Develop The Skill Of Effective Signaling In A Negotiation In Order To Get The Best Possible Outcome

- Exploring How To Get The Deal That You Want In A Negotiation: How To Develop The Skill Of Exploring What Is Possible In A Negotiation In Order To

Reach The Best Possible Deal

- Use The Power Of Arguing To Win Your Next Negotiation: How To Develop The Skill Of Effective Arguing In A Negotiation In Order To Get The Best Possible Outcome

- Learn How To Signal In Your Next Negotiation: How To Develop The Skill Of Effective Signaling In A Negotiation In Order To Get The Best Possible Outcome

- Learn The Skill Of Exploring In A Negotiation: How To Develop The Skill Of Exploring What Is Possible In A Negotiation In Order To Reach The Best Possible Deal

- Learn How To Argue In Your Next Negotiation: How To Develop The Skill Of Effective Arguing In A Negotiation In Order To Get The Best Possible Outcome|

- How To Open Your Next Negotiation: How To Start A Negotiation In Order To Get The Best Possible Outcome

- Preparing For Your Next Negotiation: What You Need To Do BEFORE A Negotiation Starts In Order

To Get The Best Possible Deal

- Learn How To Package Trades In Your Next Negotiation

- All Good Things Come To An End: How To Close A Negotiation - How To Develop The Skill Of Closing In Order To Get The Best Possible Outcome From A Negotiation

- Take No Prisoners In Your Next Negotiation: How To Start A Negotiation In Order To Get The Best Possible Outcome

Miscellaneous

- How To Heal A Broken Leg – Fast!: Understanding how to deal with a broken leg in order to start walking again quickly

- How Software Defined Networking (SDN) Is Going To Change Your World Forever: The Revolution In Network Design And How It Affects You

- The Power Of Virtualization: How It Affects Memory, Servers, and Storage: The Revolution In Creating Virtual Devices And How It Affects You

- The Internet-Enabled Successful School District Superintendent: How To Use The Internet To Boost Parental Involvement In Your Schools

- Power Distribution Unit (PDU) Secrets: What Everyone Who Works In A Data Center Needs To Know!

- Making The Jump: How To Land Your Dream Job When You Get Out Of College!

- How To Use The Internet To Create Successful Students And Involved Parents

"What tools to use to create your next speech so that your message will be remembered forever!

This book has been written with one goal in mind – to show you how you can use tools to create your next speech so that it will be a success. We're going to show you what you need to be doing in order to present a great speech!

Let's Make Your Next Speech A Success!

<u>What You'll Find Inside:</u>

- **CONNECT WITH YOUR AUDIENCE BY USING ENTHUSIASM**

- **CREATING HIGH QUALITY "A'S" FOR Q&AS**

- **3 REASONS WHY SPEAKERS FAIL**

- **MISTAKES THAT WE SPEAKERS MAKE**

Dr. Jim Anderson brings his 25 years of real-world experience to this book. He's delivered speeches at some of the world's largest firms as well as at many conferences. He's going to show you what you need to do in order to make your next speech a success!